T0198409

THE STORY
of
JIMMY CHIN

The little christmas tree, who could not wait for spring

CHARLENE THOMAS

To order additional copies of this book, contact:
Xlibris
844-714-8691
www.Xlibris.com
Orders@Xlibris.com

ISBN: Softcover   978-1-6641-6393-5
         EBook   978-1-6641-6394-2

Print information available on the last page

Rev. date: 03/26/2021

THE STORY

of

JIMMY CHIN

Introduction

The main goal of this book is to help the reader; BE YOUR OWN KIND OF BEAUTIFUL!

Each of us has a self-deep within and an outer self that we show the world.

What I have learned and want to share is that no matter what we are dealing with in life, the closer our inner and outer selves align the more peace, strength, calm, confidence and self-esteem we will experience.

This is the story about a young Christmas tree and his journey to be true to himself, to know it was ok to be his own kind of beautiful and therefore align his inner and outer self.

It is a journey of choice and courage.

There was a great space between who Jimmy Chin believed he was and who the world told him he was supposed to be.

It speaks of his journey from hiding himself ....to being himself.

It highlights the freedom that comes with making the choice to be yourself ...and the awareness of the power of knowing we have choice.

HIS journey takes risk and courage and the result is a self that Is happier and wiser and what surprises Jimmy most of all was the number of others who because of him found their own courage to be the self within.

The GOAL OF THIS INTERACTIVE STORY IS TO ASSIST CHILDREN IN GETTING INTOUCH WITH THEIR INNER SELVES, AND TO HELP THEM REALIZE AND EXPERIENCE SUCH TRUTHS AS:

IT IS OK TO BE WHO YOU REALLY ARE

YOU WILL HAVE SUPPORT ALONG THE WAY

HAPPINESS IS GREATER WHEN YOU ARE TRUE TO YOURSELF

The PROCESS There are discussion questions to assist teachers, parents and care givers in exploring the key concepts of Jimmy Chin's Journey to find himself.

When the reader relates to Jimmy Chin and the key message THAT IT IS OK TO BE YOURSELF AND YOUR OWN KIND OF BEAUTIFUL there are questions to help them move from the story of Jimmy Chin to their story ....to find their self-deep within.

Chapter One

Jimmy Chin came from a long line of Christmas trees When Wendy wind would stir the air the rustling would start and stories would be shared.

Stories about the Christmas trees who had travelled abroad. like representing Nova Scotia every year. In Boston to thank the city for their help in the Halifax explosion. There were stories of being dressed up for first family events and being decorated for great balls and being the main attraction at Church halls,

Jimmy Chin heard these stories and many more and it was the stories that gave him the sense of just what being a Christmas was all about, he pondered all of this in heart.

Jimmy learned that "real" Christmas trees loved winter and the white fluffy snowy jackets they often wore and the fancy bells and lights made them smile even more. He learned what every Christmas tree knew for sure that Christmas trees thought and dreamed of Winter and that no other season counted for more. And here is where young Jimmy Chin kept a secret deep within and it made him feel like he couldn't fit in because he was the Christmas tree who couldn't wait for spring.

Chapter Two

It was not easy for young Jimmy Chin to know he was different deep down within.

Some of the Christmas trees stayed home in the forest and with time they became the elders, the best rustle story tellers the wisest of all the Christmas trees.

Jimmy Chin sometimes thought about talking to the Christmas Tree Elders but mostly he thought about Spring. And when he did his branches would rise higher and a gentle rustle like a giggle could be heard for miles around,

Jimmy Chin loved how light he felt in spring. He loved how the spring sun helped him shed his old skin and how those needles would help warm the ground. He loved how that would help Greeny Grass abound. He saw how Greeny grass would then catch the rain and help feed his roots and he would be strong again,

And Jimmy Chin had many such memories the beauty of all the Billy Birds who played in his branches and the thank you songs they would sing. How could anybody not dream of Spring?

Jimmy Chin felt a stranger to himself when he found himself agreeing that winter was the only season for a Christmas tree to care about even agreeing that it would be grand if indeed it was a late Spring.

He felt he shouldn't couldn't call himself a real Christmas tree He felt bad about thinking and loving spring he felt there was something wrong with him and that he had better keep his secrets deep within.

It was not that Christmas tree live was all bad. Jimmy did have Spring seasons to embrace and he saw his fellow saplings grow strong and green and the Elder Rustle stories were shared all the time and over time he even had a few stories to spin but deep inside he still thought of Spring.

He would think about the lives of his ancestor trees. Their bravery to be who they really were whether that be the tree at the Mall or the old country Hall or remain standing in the forest to be the guide for them all, He thought about their choices and how even when others couldn't understand they stood firm in their own power which made them quite grand.

In a moment of clear thinking he recognized that the very trees who seemed to be too bold became the hero whenever Rustle stories were told.

In that moment of Jimmy Chin knew what he had to do. He knew in his root of roots that while some Christmas Trees would not understand others would applaud him being true to the self within .... maybe it was alright to think about Spring.

He suddenly felt lighter than he had since ...since well ever and he thought and it is not even Spring

I AM MAKING MY OWN SPRING

I AM MAKING MY OWN SPRING

Was the song that kept rising from deep within

And before you could say Christmas tree Wendy Wind joined in and Jimmy Chin sang in his loudest

Rustle I am making my own Spring. I am making my own Spring

It was time to talk to the Elders he knew to his self-deep within it was time to be true.

The Christmas tree Elders listened quietly which was their style and then they rustled to Jimmy to listen for a while.

"It doesn't matter if you love Spring. it doesn't matter at all"

"It only matters that you love who you are, and that you love all"

Jimmy Chin could not believe what he was hearing.

It didn't matter that most Christmas trees loved to dress and be in Winter. It didn't matter that most Christmas trees followed in the role of their ancestors.

It only mattered that he be true to himself. the self he had kept hidden deep within.

It was the very first time Jimmy Chin thought that being different was a positive thing.

Jimmy Chin smiled his biggest smile in years. He had come out from that lonely dark place he had carried even while in the sun. He had shown courage like the others Christmas trees who had chosen their own path before him. He had gained a knowing deep down within that he was exactly who he was meant to be.

He was Jimmy Chin the little Christmas tree who couldn't wait for spring.

Chapter Three

Jimmy thought about how some of his likes and dreams were different than his friends and relatives, His dreams seemed closer to his young birch friends who like him could not wait for spring.

Jimmy knew in his root of roots that some Christmas trees would not understand. Some of his family and friends would see how brave it was to speak to the Elders about his truth Some would more than welcome the "real" Jimmy Chin, some would stay in touch others not so much. But what really surprised Jimmy Chin was the number of other Christmas who also couldn't wait for spring.

It made his heart sing the number of others who had also kept in their hearts their love of spring.

Sometimes he thought when you take a risk it gives not only you but others the strength to be themselves he smiled and rested in that truth.

Jimmy recognized that each day he had a choice to make chose to be "real" or chose to be "a stranger to himself"

He chose to be real to his inner most self

Be real to the hater's in spite of themselves

He would be real to the trees who still kept their secrets within

And real to those who were different than him

You see Jimmy Chin recognized having learned HOW TO RELY ON HIMSELF TO HAVE THE GREATEST LIFE OF ALL.

BE YOURSELF, LOVE YOURSELF

WHETHER YOU ARE SHORT, BIG OR TALL

LEAN INTO WHO YOU ARE DEEP WITHIN

DON'T HIDE OR FEAR A FALL

BECAUSE BEING TRUE TO YOURSELF IS THE GREATEST GIFT OF ALL.

Chapter Four

So Jimmy Chin settled into his new self and because of it his new fife.

There were so many new experiences like he found it easier to rustle loudly when he heard stories he liked and just as loudly when there were stones he had different opinion.

He discovered that most trees liked him being himself and that for those who no longer liked him he could decide not to let them make him too upset.

He heard the Elder trees talking about him, he could hardly image. they knew his name! and they were saying he was going to make a great elder leader someday.

It was hard for Jimmy to think about that those future some days because his todays were now so full of life of giggling and learning and most of all of being himself and besides in Just three weeks it would be Spring.

EMPOWERMENT QUESTIONS UNDERSTANDING JIMMY CHIN

TO HELP ME UNDERSTAND MYSELF THAT SELF DEEP WITHIN.

1a. What was the difference between Jimmy and the other Christmas tree?

1b. What are some of the differences between you and your family and friends?

2a. Why did Jimmy pretend to like Winter the best of all?

2b. Do you ever pretend to like things you do not like?

3a. Why did Jimmy think he had to hide his love of Spring?

3b. Do you ever feel you have to hide what you love or like to do?

4a. Why was Jimmy nervous to talk to the Elder trees?

4b. Are you ever nervous to talk to the grow ups in your life?

5a. How did Jimmy feel when he talked to the Elders?

5b. How do you feel when you talk to grownups?

6. What did Jimmy learn from the Elders?

7. What was the best thing that happened for Jimmy when he talked to the Elders?

8. What did he learn about himself once he started to be himself?

9. What did Jimmy mean when he sang "I am making my own spin?"

10. Why was Jimmy happier when he told others he liked Spring?

11. Everyone did not understand Jimmy's love of Spring. Do you think it is better to be yourself even though someone may not understand or like it?

TRUE OR FALSE

1. Jimmy Chin learned that what he liked and who he was deep inside? TRUE OR FALSE

2. When Jimmy hide what he liked he felt alone and that no one would understand. TRUE OR FALSE

3. Jimmy learned that it was only ok to be himself if the other Christmas trees liked it and understand. TRUE OR FALSE

4. Jimmy Chin learned that becoming the best Christmas tree he could be takes time and that is ok. TRUE OR FALSE

Those discussing the journey of Jimmy Chin can come with other questions or true and false questions to help generalize the key points of being yourself is not always easy but in the end it makes you happiest to be who you are meant to be.

Printed in the United States
by Baker & Taylor Publisher Services